FROM
༄

DATE
༄

HELEN STEINER RICE

A COLLECTION OF
Christmas Poetry

Teal Press

Published in the UK by Teal Press Ltd.

ISBN: 978-0-99560-255-7

This English-language edition issued by special arrangement with:
Barbour Publishing, Inc.,
P.O. Box 719
Uhrichsville, Ohio, U.S.A.

©2014 by Barbour Publishing, Inc.
Compiled by Linda Hang.

A CIP catalogue record for this book is available from the British Library.

Acknowledgements:

All scripture quotations are taken from the King James Version of the Bible.

Cover Photo used under license from Shutterstock.com.

Contents

❧

❧

Helen Steiner Rice

Introduction

We call it the most wonderful time of the year. Children make their wish lists months in advance, and by mid-November shoppers are swarming the stores. Christmas music floods the airwaves, and trees with their festive decorations go up all over town. There are programs and cantatas, parties and fun going on everywhere we look. Yes, it's all quite amazing.

Even more amazing is that all these activities and preparations culminate in one small twenty-four-hour period. Sometimes, people get what they want out of the day; and more often, they don't.

How much better would it be to share the Christmas spirit all year long? That's the question hidden in Helen Steiner Rice's beautiful poetry. Imagine what a wonderful year that would be!

Let Us Live Christmas Every Day

Christmas is more than a day at the end of the year,
More than a season of joy and good cheer,
Christmas is really God's pattern for living
To be followed all year by unselfish giving ...
For the holiday season awakens good cheer
And draws us closer to those we hold dear,
And we open our hearts and find it is good
To live among men as we always should ...
But as soon as the tinsel is stripped from the tree
The spirit of Christmas fades silently
Into the background of daily routine
And is lost in the whirl of life's busy scene,

Helen Steiner Rice

And all unawares we miss and forego
The greatest blessing that mankind can know ...
For if we lived Christmas each day, as we should,
And made it our aim to always do good,
We'd find the lost key to meaningful living
That comes not from getting
but from unselfish giving ...
And we'd know the great joy of peace on earth
Which was the real purpose of our Savior's birth.
For in the glad tidings of the first Christmas night
God showed us the way and the truth and the light!

Celebration

And suddenly there was with the angel a
multitude of the heavenly host praising God,
and saying, Glory to God in the highest,
and on earth peace, good will toward men.

Luke 2:13–14

Helen Steiner Rice

May Christmas Come Again and Again

Here's hoping that your Christmas
Is a time that's set apart -
A time that's filled with happiness
And sunshine in your heart ...
And may the warmth and love you give
Return to you all year
To brighten days in many ways
And fill your life with cheer!

Behold, I Bring You Good Tidings of Great Joy

Glad tidings herald the Christ child's birth -
Joy to the world and peace on earth,
Glory to God ... let all men rejoice
And hearken once more to the angel's voice.
It matters not who or what you are -
All men can behold the Christmas star,
For the star that shone is shining still
In the hearts of men of peace and goodwill.
It offers the answer to every man's need,
Regardless of color or race or creed ...
So joining together in brotherly love,
Let us worship again our Father above,
And forgetting our own little selfish desires,
May we seek what the star of Christmas inspires.

❧

Helen Steiner Rice

A Christmas Prayer
of Praise

Praise God, the holy One,
For giving us His only Son
To live on earth as mortals do
To draw us closer, God, to You.
Praise the Father for all things
And for the message Christmas brings.
This is indeed the day of days
To raise your voice in prayers of praise -
For we would have nowhere to go
When life has ended here below,
For redemption came and salvation was won
Through Jesus Christ, the Father's Son.

⌒

A New Year's Meditation

What better time
and what better season,
What greater occasion
or more wonderful reason
To kneel down in prayer
and lift our hands high
To the God of creation,
who made earth and sky,
Who sent us His Son
to live here among men -
And the message He brought
is as true now as then ...

Helen Steiner Rice

The Christmas Story

A star in the sky, an angel's voice
Telling the world - Rejoice! Rejoice!
Shepherds tending their flocks by night,
Falling in awe at this wondrous sight,
Wise men traveling across the lands
To place their gifts in the Christ child's hands,
No room at the inn, so a manger bed
Cradled in radiance the holy babe's head ...
That is the story that's living still
In the hearts of all men.

Joy

Whom having not seen, ye love; in whom,
though now ye see him not, yet believing,
ye rejoice with joy unspeakable and full of glory.

1 Peter 1:8

Helen Steiner Rice

May the Star Shine in Your Heart

May the holy remembrance
of that first Christmas night
Make this blessed season
more joyous and bright ...
And may the star of Bethlehem,
which shone down from above,
Keep shining in your heart today
and in the hearts of those you love.

More Christmas Wishes

At Christmas may God grant you
Special gifts of joy and cheer,
And bless you for the good you do
For others through the year ...
May you find rich satisfaction
In your daily work and prayer,
And in knowing as you serve Him
He will keep you in His care.

Helen Steiner Rice

I Am the Light of the World

In this sick world of hatred
and violence and sin,
Where society renounces morals
and rejects discipline,
We stumble in darkness
groping vainly for light
To distinguish the difference
between wrong and right ...
But dawn cannot follow
this night of despair
Unless faith lights a candle
in all hearts everywhere ...
And warmed by the glow,
our hate melts away
And love lights the path
to a peaceful new day.

A New Year's Meditation

What better time
and what better season,
What greater occasion
or more wonderful reason
To kneel down in prayer
and lift our hands high
To the God of creation,
who made earth and sky,
Who sent us His Son
to live here among men -
And the message He brought
is as true now as then ...

Helen Steiner Rice

A Christmas Prayer
for Joy

Our Father, who art in heaven,
hear this Christmas prayer,
And if it be Thy gracious will,
may joy be everywhere -
The joy that comes from knowing
that the holy Christ child came
To bless the earth at Christmas
for Thy sake and in Thy name.
And with this prayer there comes a wish,
that these holy, happy days
Will bless your loved ones everywhere
in many joyous ways.

Giving

Every man shall give as he is able, according
to the blessing of the Lord thy God
which he hath given thee.

Deuteronomy 16:17

Helen Steiner Rice

The Spirit of Giving

Each year at Christmas, the spirit of giving
Adds joy to the season and gladness to living.
Knowing this happens when Christmas is here,
Why can't we continue throughout the year
To make our lives happy and abundant with living
By following each day the spirit of giving?

Gifts from God

This brings you a million good wishes and more
For the things you cannot buy in a store -
Like faith to sustain you in times of trial,
A joy-filled heart and a happy smile,
Contentment, inner peace, and love -
All priceless gifts from God above!

The Gift of God's Love

All over the world at this season,
expectant hands reach to receive
Gifts that are lavishly fashioned -
the finest that man can conceive ...
For purchased and given at Christmas
are luxuries we long to possess,
Given as favors and tokens
to try in some way to express
That strange, indefinable feeling
which is part of this glad time of year
When streets are crowded with shoppers
and the air resounds with good cheer ...

Helen Steiner Rice

But back of each tinsel-tied package
exchanged at this gift-giving season,
Unrecognized often by many,
lies a deeper, more meaningful reason -
For born in a manger at Christmas
as a gift from the Father above,
An infant whose name was called Jesus
brought mankind the gift of God's love ...
And the gifts that we give have no purpose
unless God is part of the giving
And unless we make Christmas a pattern
to be followed in everyday living.

The Priceless Gift
of Christmas

Now Christmas is a season
for joy and merrymaking,
A time for gifts and presents,
for giving and for taking,
A festive, friendly, happy time
when everyone is gay -
But have we ever really felt
the greatness of the day?
For through the centuries the world
has wandered far away
From the beauty and the meaning
of the holy Christmas Day ...
For Christmas is a heavenly gift
that only God can give -
It's ours just for the asking
for as long as we shall live ...

Helen Steiner Rice

It can't be bought or bartered,
it can't be won or sold,
It doesn't cost a penny,
and it's worth far more than gold.
It isn't bright and gleaming
for eager eyes to see—
It can't be wrapped in tinsel
or placed beneath a tree.
It isn't soft and shimmering
for reaching hands to touch,
Or some expensive luxury
you've wanted very much.
For the priceless gift of Christmas
is meant just for the heart,
And we receive it only
when we become a part

Of the kingdom and the glory
which is ours to freely take,
For God sent the holy Christ child
at Christmas for our sake
So man might come to know Him
and feel His presence near
And see the many miracles
performed when He was here.
And this priceless gift of Christmas
is within the reach of all—
The rich, the poor, the young and old,
the greatest and the small.
So take His priceless gift of love—
reach out and you receive—
And the only payment that God asks
is just that you believe.

Christmas Is a Season for Giving

Christmas is a season
for gifts of every kind -
All the glittery, pretty things
that Christmas shoppers find -
Baubles, beads, and bangles
of silver and of gold -
Anything and everything
that can be bought or sold
Is given at this season
to place beneath the tree,
For Christmas is a special time
for giving lavishly.
But there's one rare and priceless gift
that can't be sold or bought -
It's something poor or rich can give,
for it's a loving thought ...
And loving thoughts are blessings
for which no one can pay,
And only loving hearts can give
this priceless gift away.

Beyond Our Asking

More than hearts can imagine
or minds comprehend,
God's bountiful gifts
are ours without end.
We ask for a cupful
when the vast sea is ours,
We pick a small rosebud
from a garden of flowers,
We reach for a sunbeam
but the sun still abides,
We draw one short breath
but there's air on all sides,
Whatever we ask for
falls short of God's giving,
For His greatness exceeds
every facet of living.
And always God's ready
and eager and willing

Helen Steiner Rice

To pour out His mercy,
completely fulfilling
All of man's needs
for peace, joy, and rest,
For God gives His children
whatever is best.
Just give Him a chance
to open His treasures,
And He'll fill your life with
unfathomable pleasures -
Pleasures that never grow
worn out and faded
And leave us depleted,
disillusioned and jaded -
For God has a storehouse
just filled to the brim
With all that man needs,
if we'll only ask Him.

The Blessings of Sharing

Only what we give away
Enriches us from day to day,
For not in getting but in giving
Is found the lasting joy of living,
For no one ever had a part
In sharing treasures of the heart
Who did not feel the impact of
The magic mystery of God's love.
And love alone can make us kind
And give us joy and peace of mind,
So live with joy unselfishly
And you'll be blessed abundantly.

Helen Steiner Rice

Giving Is the Key to Living

Christmas is a season of giving
And giving is the key to living ...
So let us give ourselves away,
Not just today but every day,
And remember, a kind and thoughtful deed
Or a hand outstretched in a time of need
Is the rarest of gifts, for it is a part
Not of the purse but a loving heart ...
And he who gives of himself will find
True joy of heart and peace of mind.

Heart Gifts

It's not the things that can be bought
That are life's richest treasures,
It's just the little "heart gifts"
That money cannot measure.
A cheerful smile, a friendly word,
A sympathetic nod,
All priceless little treasures
From the storehouse of our God.
They are the things that can't be bought
With silver or with gold,
For thoughtfulness and kindness
And love are never sold.
They are the priceless things in life
For which no one can pay,
And the giver finds rich recompense
In giving them away.

Helen Steiner Rice

Give Lavishly!
Live Abundantly!

The more you give, the more you get
The more you laugh, the less you fret.
The more you do unselfishly,
The more you live abundantly.
The more of everything you share,
The more you'll always have to spare.
The more you love, the more you'll find
That life is good and friends are kind,
For only what we give away
Enriches us from day to day.
So let's live Christmas through the year
And fill the world with love and cheer.

A Gift of Joy

As once more we approach the birthday of our King,
Do we search our hearts for a gift we can bring?
Do we stand by in awe like the small drummer boy
Who had no rare jewels, not even a toy
To lay at Christ's crib like the wise men of old,
Who brought precious gifts of silver and gold?
But the drummer boy played for the infant child,
And the baby Jesus looked up and smiled,
For the boy had given the best he had,
And his gift from the heart made the Savior glad.
Today He still smiles on all those who bring
Their hearts to lay at the feet of the King.

Helen Steiner Rice

Prayer

Give, and it shall be given unto you; good
measure, pressed down, and shaken together,
and running over, shall men give into your bosom.
For with the same measure that ye mete withal
it shall be measured to you again.

Luke 6:38

Helen Steiner Rice

May Christmas Renew in Us a Childlike Faith

May Christmas renew in us a childlike faith
For only then can we all endure
These changing times and feel secure,
For faith in things we cannot see
Requires a child's simplicity -
For in a small child's shining eyes
The faith of all the ages lies ...
And tiny hands and tousled heads
That kneel in prayer by little beds
Are closer to the dear Lord's heart
And of His kingdom more a part
Than we who search and never find
The answer to our questioning minds -
For God can never be defined
By any meager, mortal mind,
And only a child can completely accept
What probing adults research and reject.
O Father, grant once more to men
A simple, childlike faith again,
For only by faith and faith alone
Can we approach our Father's throne.

c~o

A Prayer for Christmas

God, give us eyes this Christmas
to see the Christmas star,
And give us ears to hear the song
of angels from afar ...
And with our eyes and ears attuned
for a message from above,
Let Christmas angels speak to us
of hope and faith and love -
Hope to light our pathway
when the way ahead is dark,
Hope to sing through stormy days
with the sweetness of a lark,
Faith to trust in things unseen
and know beyond all seeing
That it is in our Father's love
we live and have our being.

Helen Steiner Rice

God Is Always There to Hear Our Prayer

Let us find joy in the news of His birth,
And let us find comfort and strength for each day
In knowing that Christ walked this same earthly way,
So He knows all our needs
and He hears every prayer,
And He keeps all His children
always safe in His care ...
And whenever we're troubled and lost in despair,
We have but to seek Him and ask Him in prayer
To guide and direct us and help us to bear
Our sickness and sorrow, our worry and care ...
So once more at Christmas
let the whole world rejoice
In the knowledge He answers
every prayer that we voice.

Listen in Silence
If You Would Hear

Let us listen in silence so we may hear
The Christmas message more clearly this year.
Silently the green leaves grow;
In silence falls the soft, white snow ...
Silently bright stars appear,
In silence velvet night draws near.
And silently God enters in
To free a troubled heart from sin,
For God works silently in lives,
And nothing spiritual survives
Amid the din of a noisy street
Where raucous crowds with hurrying feet
And blinded eyes and deafened ears
Are never privileged to hear
The message God wants to impart
To every troubled, weary heart.
So let not our worldly celebrations
Disturb our Christmas meditations,
For only in a quiet place
Can we behold God face-to-face.

❧

Helen Steiner Rice

Learn to Rest

We all need short vacations
in life's fast and maddening race -
An interlude of quietness
from the constant, jet-age pace,
So when your day is pressure-packed
and your hours are all too few
Just close your eyes and meditate
and let God talk to you.

A Christmas Prayer

Oh God, in Thy great goodness,
May our guidance Christmas night
Be the star the wise men followed -
Not a man-made satellite.

Friends & Family

A man that hath friends must shew himself
friendly: and there is a friend that sticketh
closer than a brother.

Proverbs 18:24

Helen Steiner Rice

Christmastime Is
Friendship Time

At Christmastime our hearts reach out
to friends we think of dearly,
And checking through our friendship lists,
as all of us do yearly,
We stop awhile to reminisce
and to pleasantly review
Happy little happenings
and things we used to do ...
And though we've been too busy
to keep in touch all year,
We send a Christmas greeting
at this season of good cheer ...
So Christmas is a lovely link
between old years and new
That keeps the bond of friendship
forever unbroken and true.

෴

Why Write These Christmas Greetings?

I wonder if you know the real reason
I send you a card every year at this season?
Do you think it's a habit I just can't break
Or something I do just for custom's sake?
I think I should tell you it's something more
For to me Christmas opens the friendship door ...
And I find myself reaching across the year
And clasping the hand of somebody dear.
To me it's a link I wouldn't want broken
That holds us together when words are unspoken.
For often through the year we have to forego
Exchanging good wishes with those we know,
But Christmas opens the door of the heart
And whether we're close or far apart ...
When I write your name I think of you
And pause and reflect and always renew
The bond that exists since we first met
And I found you somebody too nice to forget.

࿐

Helen Steiner Rice

Christmas Thanks

❧

This comes to you with loving thoughts
When Christmastime is here -
Thoughts of all the qualities
That make you very dear ...
And this brings you many wishes
That today and always, too,
You'll have the special happiness
That ought to come to you.

❧

A Christmas Wish

❧

At Christmas and always,
May you be guided by His light
And surrounded with His love.

❧

Every Year When Christmas Comes

I have a list of folks I know
all written in a book
And every year when Christmas comes,
I go and take a look.
And that is when I realize
that these names are a part
Not of the book they're written in,
but of my very heart.
And while it sounds fantastic
for me to make this claim
I really feel that I'm composed
of each remembered name,
So never think my Christmas cards
are just a mere routine

Helen Steiner Rice

Of names upon a Christmas list
forgotten in between,
For I am but the total
of the many folks I've met,
And you happen to be one of those
I prefer to not forget.
And every year when Christmas comes,
I realize anew
The best gift life can offer
is meeting folks like you -
And may the spirit of Christmas
that forevermore endures
Leave its richest blessings
in the hearts of you and yours.

Greeting Friends

It's Christmas and time to greet you once more,
But what can I say that I've not said before
Except to repeat at this meaningful season
That I have a deeply significant reason
For sending this greeting to tell you today
How thankful I am that you passed my way.

A Favorite Recipe

Take a cup of kindness, mix it well with love,
Add a lot of patience and faith in God above.
Sprinkle very generously
with joy and thanks and cheer -
And you'll have lots of "angel food"
to feast on all the year.

Helen Steiner Rice

Hush-a-Bye, Honey

Hush-a-bye, hush-a-bye, my sleepy head,
Angels are waiting to tuck you in bed.
Go to sleep, go to sleep, close your bright eyes,
Nighttime is tumbling out of the skies.
Angels are waiting their vigil to keep,
The sandman is filling your wee eyes with sleep.
Hush-a-bye, baby, hush-a-bye, sweet,
Playtime is over for tired, tiny feet.
Close your eyes, honey, sleepy time's here,
Good night, little darling, good night, little dear.

A New Year's Meditation

At this glad season, when there's joy everywhere,
Let us meet our Redeemer at the altar of prayer,
Asking Him humbly to bless all of our days
And grant us forgiveness for our erring ways ...
And though we're unworthy, dear Father above,
Accept us today and let us dwell in Thy love
So we may grow stronger upheld by Thy grace,
And with Thy assistance be ready to face
All the temptations that fill every day,
And hold on to our hands when we stumble and stray ...
And thank You, dear God, for the year that now ends
And for the great blessing of loved ones and friends.

Helen Steiner Rice

Widen My Vision

God, open my eyes so I may see
And feel Your presence close to me.
Give me strength for my stumbling feet
As I battle the crowd on life's busy street,
And widen the vision of my unseeing eyes
So in passing faces I'll recognize
Not just a stranger, unloved and unknown,
But a friend with a heart that is much like my own.
Give me perception to make me aware
That scattered profusely on life's thoroughfare
Are the best gifts of God that we daily pass by
As we look at the world with an unseeing eye.

The Meaning of Christmas

And the Word was made flesh, and dwelt among us,
(and we beheld his glory, the glory as of the only
begotten of the Father,) full of grace and truth.

John 1:14

Helen Steiner Rice

This Is the Savior of the World

All the world has heard the story
of the little Christ child's birth,
But too few have felt the meaning
of His mission here on earth.
Some regard the Christmas story
as something beautiful to hear,
A lovely Christmas custom
that we celebrate each year,
But it is more than just a story told
to make our hearts rejoice -
It's our Father up in heaven speaking
through the Christ child's voice,
Telling us of heavenly kingdoms
that He has prepared above
For all who trust His mercy
and live only for His love ...
And only through the Christ child
can man be born again,
for God sent the baby Jesus
as the Savior of all men.

༄

The Comfort of His Love

A baby was born in a manger
While a bright star shone down from above,
And the world learned the depths of God's mercy
And the comfort and strength of His love.
May the thought of that long ago Christmas
And the meaning it's sure to impart,
Bring a wonderful message of comfort
And a deep new peace to your heart.

Helen Steiner Rice

The Miracle of Christmas

❧

The wonderment in a small child's eyes,
The ageless awe in the Christmas skies,
The nameless joy that fills the air,
The throngs that kneel in praise and prayer -
These are the things that make us know
That men may come and men may go,
But none will ever find a way
To banish Christ from Christmas Day,
For with each child there's born again
A mystery that baffles men.

❧

The Christmas Story

Some regard the Christmas story
as something beautiful to hear -
A dramatized tradition
that's retold from year to year,
But it is more than just a story -
it's God's promise to all men
That only through the Christ child
can man be born again.
It's God's assurance of a future
beyond all that man has dreamed ...

Helen Steiner Rice

For Jesus lived on earth and died
so that man might be redeemed -
And eternal is the kingdom
that God has prepared above
For all who trust His mercy
and dwell daily in His love.
Mankind's hope and his salvation
are in the Christmas story,
For in these words there are revealed
God's greatness and His glory.

Only with Our Hearts

With our eyes we see
The glitter of Christmas,
With our ears we hear
Its merriment,
With our hands we touch
The tinsel-tied trinkets ...
But only with our hearts can we feel
The miracle of it.

A Christmas Message

Love is the message
that was sent to earth
On that first holy Christmas
that heralded Christ's birth!

Helen Steiner Rice

A Prayer for Christmas Every Day

Oh Father up in heaven,
we have wandered far away
From the little holy Christ child
that was born on Christmas Day,
And the peace on earth You promised
we have been unmindful of,
Not believing we could find it
in a simple thing called love.
We've forgotten why You sent us
Jesus Christ, Your only Son,
And in arrogance and ignorance
it's our will, not Thine, be done.
Oh, forgive us, heavenly Father,
teach us how to be more kind
So that we may judge all people
with our hearts and not our minds ...
Oh, forgive us, heavenly Father,
and help us to find the way
To understand each other
and live Christmas every day.

ꙅ

God Is Everywhere

Our Father up in heaven,
long, long years ago,
Looked down in His great mercy
upon the earth below
And saw that folks were lonely
and lost in deep despair,
And so He said, "I'll send My Son
to walk among them there
So they can hear Him speaking
and feel His nearness, too,
And see the many miracles
that faith alone can do ...

Helen Steiner Rice

For if man really sees Him
and can touch His healing hand,
I know it will be easier
to believe and understand."
And so the holy Christ child
came down to live on earth,
And that is why we celebrate
His holy, wondrous birth ...
And that is why at Christmas
the world becomes aware
That heaven may seem far away,
but God is everywhere.

What Is Christmas?

Is it just a day at the end of the year -
A season of joy, merrymaking, and cheer?
Is it people and presents and glittering trees?
Oh no, it is more than any of these,
For under the tinsel and hidden from sight
Is the promise and meaning
of that first Christmas night
When the shepherds stood in wondered awe
And felt transformed by what they saw.
So let us not in our search for pleasure
Forego our right to this priceless treasure,
For Christmas is still a God-given day,
And let us remember to keep it that way.

Helen Steiner Rice

Christmas and
the Christ Child

In our Christmas celebrations
of merriment and mirth,
Let us not forget the miracle
of the holy Christ child's birth ...
For in our festivities it is easy to lose sight
Of the baby in the manger
and that holy silent night ...
And we miss the mighty meaning
and we lose the greater glory
Of the holy little Christ child
and the blessed Christmas story
If we don't keep Christ in Christmas
and make His love a part
Of all the joy and happiness
that fill our homes and hearts.

∾

The Presence of Jesus

Jesus came into this world
one glorious Christmas Eve.
He came to live right here on earth
to help us all believe.
For God in His heaven
knew His children all would feel
That if Jesus lived among them
they would know that He was real
And not a far-off stranger
who dwelt up in the sky
And knew neither joys or sorrows
that make us laugh and cry.
And so He walked among us
and taught us how to love
And promised us that someday
we would dwell with Him above.
And while we cannot see Him
as they did, face-to-face,
We know that He is everywhere,
and not in some far-off place.

Helen Steiner Rice

Was It Really So?

Was the Christ child born in a manger-bed
Without a pillow to rest His head?
Did He walk on earth and live and die
And return to God to dwell on high?
We were not there to hear or see,
But our hopes and dreams of eternity
Are centered around that holy story
When God sent us His Son in glory -
And life on earth has not been the same,
Regardless of what the skeptics claim,
For no event ever left behind
A transformation of this kind ...
So question and search and doubt, if you will,
But the story of Christmas is living still.

Messenger of Love

Listen - be quiet -
perhaps you can hear
The Christmas tree speaking,
soft and clear:
I am God's messenger of love,
and in my Christmas dress,
I come to light your heart and home
with joy and happiness.
I bring you pretty packages
and longed-for gifts of love,
But most of all I bring you
a message from above -
The message Christmas angels sang
on that first Christmas night
When Jesus Christ, the Father's Son,
became this dark world's light.

Helen Steiner Rice

For though I'm tinsel-laden
and beautiful to see,
Remember, I am much, much more
than just a glittering tree,
More than a decoration
to enhance the Christmas scene,
I am a living symbol
that God's love is evergreen,
And when Christmas Day is over
and the holidays are through,
May the joyous spirit of Christmas
abide all year with you.
So have a merry Christmas
in the blessed Savior's name
And thank Him for the priceless gifts
that are ours because He came.

A Little Child Shall Lead Them

God sent the little Christ child
So man might understand
That a little child shall lead them
To that unknown Promised Land.
For God in His great wisdom
Knew that men would rise to power
And forget His holy precepts
In their great triumphal hour ...
He knew that they would question
And doubt the holy birth
And turn their time and talents
To the pleasures of this earth ...

Helen Steiner Rice

But every new discovery
Is an open avenue
To more and greater mysteries,
And man's search is never through ...
And man can never fathom
The mysteries of the Lord
Or understand His promise
Of a heavenly reward ...
And no one but a little child
With simple faith and love
Can lead man's straying footsteps
To higher realms above.

Blessings

And Mary said, My soul doth magnify the Lord,
And my spirit hath rejoiced in God my Saviour.
For he hath regarded the low estate of his
handmaiden: for, behold, from henceforth all
generations shall call me blessed. For he that is mighty
hath done to me great things; and holy is his name.

Luke 1:46–49

Helen Steiner Rice

A Christmas Blessing

May Jesus, our Savior,
who was born on Christmas Day,
Bless you at this season
in a very special way.
May the beauty and the promise
of that silent, holy night
Fill your heart with peace and happiness
and make your new year bright.

Wishes for This Christmas

May this Christmas season bring you
Many blessings from above,
And may the coming year be filled
With peace and joy and love.

A Christmas Prayer

God bless you at Christmas
And go with you through the year,
And whenever you are troubled
May you feel His presence near.
May the greatness of His mercy
And the sweetness of His peace
Bring you everlasting comfort
And the joys that never cease.

Helen Steiner Rice

Where There Is Love

Where there is love the heart is light,
Where there is love the day is bright ...
Love changes darkness into light
And makes the heart take wingless flight.
Oh, blessed are those who walk in love,
They also walk with God above.

Discovering Christmas

May Christmas this year, amid chaos, cruelty,
and conflict, be a blessed instrument through
which we can find comfort, courage, and cheer
in the communion of our hearts.
May we discover this Christmas, the sustaining
powers of a strong faith and the abiding
values of courage, heroism, honor,
fellowship, and freedom.
May our material gifts be less
and our spiritual gifts greater.
"Peace on earth, goodwill to all"
is not an empty dream.
It is the miracle of Christmas and such miracles
are made of faith and brave hearts.
May God bless you and may the New Year
find us all not only safe, but free.

Helen Steiner Rice

Thoughts of Thanks

࿊

At this time may God grant you
Special gifts of joy and cheer,
And bless you for the good you do
For others through the year. . .
May you find rich satisfaction
In your daily work and prayer,
And in knowing as you serve Him
He will keep you in His care.

࿊

Thank You, God, for Everything

Thank You, God, for everything -
the big things and the small -
For every good gift comes from God,
the giver of them all,
And all too often we accept
without any thanks or praise
The gifts God sends as blessings
each day in many ways.
And so at this time
we offer up a prayer
To thank You, God, for giving us
a lot more than our share.
First, thank You for the little things
that often come our way -
The things we take for granted
and don't mention when we pray -

Helen Steiner Rice

The unexpected courtesy,
the thoughtful, kindly deed,
A hand reached out to help us
in the time of sudden need.
Oh, make us more aware, dear God,
of little daily graces
That come to us with sweet surprise
from never-dreamed-of places.
Then thank You for the miracles
we are much too blind to see,
and give us new awareness
of our many gifts from Thee.
And help us to remember
that the key to life and living
Is to make each prayer a prayer of thanks
and each day a day of thanksgiving.

Showers of Blessings

Each day there are showers of blessings
sent from the Father above,
For God is a great, lavish giver,
and there is no end to His love ...
And His grace is more than sufficient,
His mercy is boundless and deep,
And His infinite blessings are countless,
and all this we're given to keep
If we but seek God and find Him
and ask for a bounteous measure
Of this wholly immeasurable offering
from God's inexhaustible treasure ...
For no matter how big man's dreams are,
God's blessings are infinitely more,
For always God's giving is greater
than what man is asking for.

Helen Steiner Rice

Peace

Blessed are the peacemakers: for they
shall be called the children of God.

Matthew 5:9

Helen Steiner Rice

A Beautiful Beginning
for Peace on Earth

Let us all remember
when our faith is running low,
Christ is more than just a figure
wrapped in an ethereal glow ...
For He came and dwelled among us
and He knows our every need,
And He loves and understands us
and forgives each sinful deed.
He was crucified and buried
and rose again in glory,
And His promise of salvation
makes the wondrous Christmas story
An abiding reassurance that
the little Christ child's birth
Was the beautiful beginning
of God's plan for peace on earth.

⌒

A Christmas Prayer

O God, our help in ages past,
our hope in years to be,
Look down upon this present
and see our need of Thee ...
For in this age of unrest,
with danger all around,
We need Thy hand to lead us
to a higher, safer ground.
We need Thy help and counsel
to make us more aware
That our safety and security
lie solely in Thy care,
And so we pray this Christmas
to feel Thy presence near
And for Thy all-wise guidance
throughout the coming year.

Helen Steiner Rice

First, give us understanding,
enough to make us kind,
So we may judge all people
with our hearts and not our minds.
Then give us strength and courage
to be honorable and true,
And place our trust implicitly
in unseen things and You ...
And help us when we falter
and renew our faith each day
And forgive our human errors
and hear us when we pray,
And keep us gently humble
in the greatness of Thy love
So someday we are fit to dwell
with Thee in peace above.

A Christmas Prayer for Peace

We pray to Thee, our Father,
as Christmas comes again,
For peace among all nations
and goodwill between all men.
Give us the strength and courage
to search ourselves inside
And recognize our vanity,
our selfishness, and pride ...
For the struggle of all ages
is centered deep within,
Where each man has his private war
that his own soul must win ...
For a world of peace and plenty,
of which all men have dreamed,
Can only be attained and kept
when the spirit is redeemed.

Helen Steiner Rice

Glory to God

Glory to God in the highest
and peace on earth to men" -
May the Christmas song the angels sang
stir in our hearts again
And bring a new awareness
that the fate of every nation
Is sealed securely in the hand
of the Maker of creation.
For man, with all his knowledge,
his inventions, and his skill,
Can never go an inch beyond
the holy Father's will,
And when we fully recognize
the helplessness of man
And seek our Father's guidance
in our every thought and plan,
Then only can we build a world
of faith and hope and love,
And only then can man achieve
the life he's dreaming of.

The Miracle of Christmas

Miracles are marvels
That defy all explanation
And Christmas is a miracle
And not just a celebration -
For when the true significance
Of this so-called Christmas story
Penetrates the minds of men
And transforms them with its glory,
Then only can rebellious man,
So hate-torn with dissension,
Behold his adversaries
With a broader new dimension -

Helen Steiner Rice

For we can only live in peace
When we learn to love each other
And accept all human beings
With the compassion of a brother -
And it takes the Christ of Christmas
To change man's point of view,
For only through the Christ child
Can all men be born anew ...
And in the Christmas story
Of the holy Christ child's birth
Is the answer to a better world
And goodwill and peace on earth.

A Season of Kindness

May the kindly spirit of Christmas
spread its radiance far and wide,
So all the world may feel the glow
of this holy Christmastide.
Then may every heart and home
continue through the year
To feel the warmth and wonder
of this season of good cheer.
And may it bring us closer
to God and to each other
Till every stranger is a friend
and every man a brother.

Helen Steiner Rice

The Fortress of Peace Within

Peace is not something you fight for
with bombs and missiles that kill -
Peace is attained in the silence
that comes when the heart stands still ...
For hearts that are restless and warlike
with longings that never cease
Can never contribute ideas
that bring the world nearer to peace ...
For as dew never falls on a morning
that follows a dark, stormy night,
The peace and grace of our Father
fall not on a soul in flight ...
So if we seek peace for all people,
there is but one place to begin,
And the armament race will not win it,
for the fortress of peace is within.

The First Christmas Morn

In this world of violence and hatred and greed
Where men lust for power and scorn those in need,
What could we hope for and where could we go
To find comfort and courage on this earth below
If in Bethlehem's manger Christ had not been born
Many centuries ago on the first Christmas morn?
For life everlasting and eternal glory
Were promised to man in the Christmas story.

Helen Steiner Rice

May You Feel the Quiet Beauty

May you feel the quiet beauty
of that holy, silent night
When God sent the little Christ child
to be this dark world's light.
May you know the peace He promised,
may you feel His presence near,
Not only just at Christmas,
but throughout a happy year.

The Prayer of Peace

Our Father up in heaven,
hear this fervent prayer -
May the people of all nations
be united in Thy care ...
For earth's peace and man's salvation
can come only by Thy grace.

Helen Steiner Rice

With His Love

If you found any beauty in the poems in this book
or some peace and comfort in a word or a line,
Don't give me the praise or the worldly acclaim,
for the words that you read are not mine.
I borrowed them all to share with you
from our heavenly Father above,
And the joy that you felt was God speaking to you
as He flooded your heart with His love.

Helen Steiner Rice